A SHORT HISTORY OF ALE

Jimmy Young

DAVID & CHARLES
Newton Abbot   London   North Pomfret (VT)

A Short History of Ale is condensed from the author's forthcoming *Encyclopaedia of Beer*.

British Library Cataloguing in Publication Data

Young, Jimmy, b. 1918
  A short history of ale.
  1. Beer—History   2. Brewing industry—
  Great Britain—History.
  I. Title
  641.2'3   TP577

  ISBN 0-7153-7839-2

Library of Congress Catalog Card Number 79–52373

Printed in Great Britain
by Biddles Limited, Guildford
for David & Charles (Publishers) Limited
Brunel House   Newton Abbot   Devon

Published in the United States of America
by David & Charles Inc
North Pomfret   Vermont 05053   USA

Did you know that Elizabeth I was a great ale-drinker; that at one time ale was drunk for breakfast; that ale was first taxed in 1643, after various unsuccessful attempts to do so earlier; that evidence of the existence of our 'national beverage' has been found as early as 3000BC? In this fascinating history of its production, sale and consumption you can see how our public houses have gradually become what they are today, how ale itself has changed over the years and when some of the great brewing families first started in the business. Anyone who ever goes inside a public house will find something of interest in this book.

3000BC Pottery found in Bronze Age burial sites has led Dr James Dickson – a leading Glasgow botanist – to the conclusion that an alcoholic beverage was in use in Scotland. Pollen found in a beaker suggests that it contained some form of honey, which was used in preparing mead.

3000–2300BC A sacrificial relief, found at Sakkara (South of Cairo) now in the Heineken Brewery, Holland, is inscribed at the top 'filling of the stone bottles with beer'. The text below reads 'putting the rest into a kettle'.

2225BC   A tablet in the British Museum refers to beerhouses near Babylon.

14th century BC   Beer was the favourite beverage of the Egyptians. It was made in a mash-tub, with barley steeped in water, and raised by fermented crumbs of bread. 'When freshly made, it was soft and pleasant to taste, but was easily disturbed and soon turned sour. To remedy this an infusion of lupin was added to the beer, giving it a certain bitterness and preserving it!' Professor Maspero, *The Thebes of Ramesis II*.

1st century AD   An ear of barley was depicted on one side of a British coin (the Cunobelin). Pliny the Elder, the Roman historian, recorded that when the Romans landed in Kent in 55BC they discovered drinks made from barley in use. He adds: 'the whole world is addicted to drunkenness; the perverted ingenuity of man has given to water the power of intoxication. Where wine is not procurable, western nations intoxicate themselves by means of moistened grain [a kind of ale].'

5th century AD   Among the members of St Patrick's household was a brewster called Mescan. In the life of St Brigid it is recorded that 'she brewed ale to supply to churches in the neighbourhood, at Easter'.

6th century AD   St Gildas the Wise decreed that 'any Monk whose speech got too thick through excess of ale, had to do 15 days penance'; the hardened toper had 40 days penance to sober him up.

668–93   Theodore, 7th Archbishop of Canterbury decreed that 'a Christian layman who drank too much would have to do 15 days penance'. (Heathens were not under his jurisdiction.)

688   Ina, King of Wessex, made laws setting up alehouses, the successors to the Roman *tabernae*.

7th century AD   Penalties were imposed for bad brewing; usually a period in the ducking seat at the village pond.

728 Laws were passed controlling booths set up on roads entering towns. This was the normal place for a tavern.

740–50 Ecbright, Archbishop of York, issued Canon No 18 ordering 'that no priest to go to eat or drink in "Taverns" '.

A punishment barrel

793 Old Fighting Cocks, St Albans, Hertfordshire, originally site of St Jermains Gate, part of a monastery founded by King Offa of Mercia. Centre for cockfighting in 17th and 18th century. Renamed Fisherman in 1849 after cockfighting made illegal.

822 Hops were recorded as growing in the Ile de France, and in Bavaria even earlier.

953 Bingley Arms, Bardsey, Leeds, first recorded. England's oldest inhabited Inn.

959–75 King Edgar (influenced by the then Archbishop of Canterbury, St Dunstan) closed many alehouses by limiting each village or small town to only 1 such house. He ordered the use of cups with pins (pegs) or nicks in them, adding a law that 'what person drank passed the pins in one draught should forfeit a penny'. The division meant that 8 draughts were approximately a quart. Thus arose the phrase 'Take him down a peg or two'.

975 It was decreed that 'there shall be one system of measurement and one standard of weights throughout the country, such as is in use in London and Winchester'.

Archbishop Dunstan issued Canon 26: 'Let no drinking be allowed in Church'; and in Canon 58 ordered that 'no priest be an alescop, nor in any wise act the gleeman'. An alescop was a musical reciter in an alehouse, a gleeman was a minstrel.

1002 'God Begot Winchester' recorded. (No longer a full on licence but a famous hospice of the middle ages).

Anglo-Saxon tumblers

1029 The Fountain, Canterbury, claims to have been in existence. If this is correct, it is the 2nd oldest pub in England.

1086 The Domesday survey: many important houses are mentioned, as well as towns and villages and their tithes. 38 vineyards are mentioned in the Domesday Book.

1102 Archbishop Anselm of Canterbury decreed that priests were not to take part in peg drinking bouts. King Edgar's decree that drinking vessels should be marked had led to a new popular pastime: contests to discover who could drink a given measure fastest.

1110 Skirrid Inn, Llanfihangel Crucorney, nr. Abergavenny, Wales, possibly the oldest original structure in Wales, standing as a pub today.

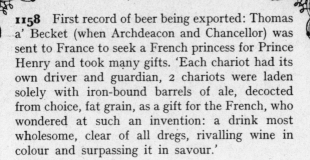

1158 First record of beer being exported: Thomas a' Becket (when Archdeacon and Chancellor) was sent to France to seek a French princess for Prince Henry and took many gifts. 'Each chariot had its own driver and guardian, 2 chariots were laden solely with iron-bound barrels of ale, decocted from choice, fat grain, as a gift for the French, who wondered at such an invention: a drink most wholesome, clear of all dregs, rivalling wine in colour and surpassing it in savour.'

1175 Archbishop Richard of Canterbury (Becket's successor) issued his Canon 3: 'Let no clerks in Holy Orders go to eat or drink in Taverns, nor be present at drinking bouts, unless on his travels. Let the offender desist or be deposed.'

1189 As a fire-prevention measure a regulation was introduced in London that stated: 'All ale-houses be forbidden, except those which shall be licensed by the Common Council of the City at Guildhall, excepting those belonging to persons who will build of stone, that the city may be secure. And that no bakers bake, or ale-wifes brew, by night, either with reeds or straw or stubble, but with wood only.'

A little later, London brewers were ordered to have their premises plastered and whitewashed inside and out.

Olde Trip to Jerusalem, Nottingham, a collecting point for the Crusaders ('Tryppe' is old English for 'Halt') being used as the Castle Brewhouse. A number of passages and tunnels from the bars lead into the castle.

1195 Archbishop Richard issued Canon 18 ordering 'that the priests abstain from public drinking bouts in taverns . . .'

12th century The Brewer's Company was formed in the name of Guild of our Lady and St Thomas a' Becket, who were the patron saints.

1212 The Abbot of Battle was recorded selling cider, a luxury drink at that time.

1215 Magna Carta mentioned standardization of drink measures: 'Let there be one measure of wine throughout our realm, and one measure of ale' . . . to wit the 'London quarter'. Magna Carta: 35

1248 An Act of Edward I's reign stated: 'If an Innkeeper keep his house open after curfew, he shall put on his surety for the first time his hanap [his set of measures] of the Tavern. He will forfeit for any second offence' [meaning he could no longer sell liquor].

1256 Giles of Bridport, Bishop of Salisbury, forbade the drinking of scot-ale and ordered the priests under his jurisdiction to close the forest houses.

1266 Price control: in the 51st year of Henry III's reign a statute was passed establishing the price of ale throughout England. 'When a quarter of wheat was sold for 3/– or 3/4d, or 24d and a quarter of oats for 15d, brewers in cities could afford to sell two gallons of ale for 1d and out of the cities three gallons for a penny: and when in a town [burgs] three gallons are sold for a penny, out of a town they may, and ought to sell four'.

1272 Maidshead, Tombland, Norwich, claims to be Britain's longest continuous Hospice, being the site of the 11th century Bishops Palace (remains from this date can be seen in the cellars).

1277 The first restriction on the brewer defined his measures; at the Assize of Bread and Ale it was decreed that 'No Brewster henceforth to sell except by true measures, the gallon, the pottle and the quart, to be marked by the Seal of the Alderman, and that the tun be of 150 gallons and sealed. The same Assize went on to comment on the clothing worn by the brewsters, who were dressing above their station in life: 'No woman of the Tavern shall henceforth go to market, nor into the highway out of her house with a hood furred with budge [lamb] upon forfeiting her hood to the use of Sherriffs, except dames who wear furred caps, the hoods of which bear fur such as they wish. And whereas brewsters, nurses, other servants and women of disreputable character adorn themselves and wear hoods after the manner of reputable women . . .'

1283 The Brewers' Assize of Bristol endorsed the 1266 Statute and warned that any brewsters or ale vendors contravening the set prices might be responsible for bringing punishment upon the town itself.

1292 First record of a Brewers' Society: they lodged a complaint against the Sheriffs.

1295 First record of brewing by monks at Burton-on-Trent. 'Matilda they granted her daily for life two white loaves from the Monastry, two gallons of the Convent beer, and one penny, besides seven gallons of beer for the men and other considerations.'

1305 First record of a brewer being fined for failing to pay a levy: William Saleman and his wife were fined 2/– by the ale-conner for keeping a brewery in Cornhill, London.

1309 Restrictions were introduced for keeping the peace in London: no Taverner was to keep his tavern open for wine or beer after curfew, nor

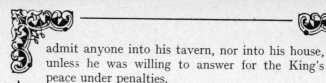

admit anyone into his tavern, nor into his house, unless he was willing to answer for the King's peace under penalties.

There were 354 taverns and 1334 alehouses where ale was brewed in London.

1327 In Faversham, Kent, 84 out of 252 registered traders were brewers: this was common throughout the country. Beer was the chief drink for breakfast, dinner, and supper, so the sale of beer developed rapidly as towns grew up; in country areas, every man brewed for his own household.

1329 Restricted hours were imposed even in the Middle Ages, if only to prevent thieves having a place of retreat. It was proclaimed in London: 'Whereas misdoers, going about by night, have their resort more in Taverns than elsewhere, and there seek refuge and watch their hour for misdoing, we forbid that any Taverner or Brewer keep the door of his Tavern open after the hour of curfew'.

1340 Queen's College, Oxford was founded and a brewer was appointed. This is the oldest brewery in England, probably the oldest in the world. It operated continuously until 1939.

1348–9 The Black Death caused a shortage of labour and, consequently, a rise in wages. Those who survived the plague no longer drank the half-penny ale, but could afford the 'Beste and Brouneste the Brewsters could brew'. (*Piers Plowman*, William Langland).

1349 A bill was passed compelling brewers to charge reasonable prices for ale, or to refund double the charge.

1353 Magistrates were charged to inquire into the 'deeds and outrages' of hosteliers and to deal summarily with them.

1368 The Mayor of the City of London ordained that 'No regratres [middle-men] shall buy ale of anyone to sell again by retail on pain of forfeiture and that the Vendor forfeit the value of the ale so sold and suffer imprisonment.'

From the Luttrel Psalter

1375 An ordinance was passed ordering all taverners of the City of London that 'no one should have an ale stake bearing his sign or leaves projecting or extending over the King's Highway, more than 7ft in length at the utmost'. The penalty for contravention was a fine of 40d to be paid to the Chamber of Guildhall.

1377 An oath was administered to ale-conners of the City of London. After reciting details about the pricing of ale, the oath continues 'You shall swear that you shall know of no Brewer or Brewster who sells . . . ale . . . otherwise than by measures sealed and full of clear ale . . . and that as soon as you shall be so required to taste any ale . . . shall be ready to do the same; and in case it be less good than it used to be before this cry, you, by assent of your Alderman, shall set a reasonable price thereon, according to your discretion; and if anyone shall afterwards see the same above the same price, unto your said Alderman you shall certify the same . . . nor when you are required to taste ale shall absent yourself without reasonable cause and true; but all things which unto your office pertain to do, you shall well and lawfully do. So God help you and the saints.'

> A nose he had that can show
> What liquor he love I trow
> For he had before long seven years
> Been of the town the ale-conner.
> (*The Cobbler of Canterbury*)

[11]

1385 An Act confirmed the 1248 one and decreed: 'if a Tavern Keeper keep his house open after curfew he shall be put on his surety the first time by his hanap of the Tavern, or by some other good pledge therein.' A second offence meant that his licence was withdrawn.

> For this gross fault I here do damn thy licence,
> Forbidding thee ever to tap or draw;
> For instantly I will in mine own person,
> Command the Constables to pull down thy sign.
>   Philip Massinger, *A New Way to Pay Old Debts*

A Mediæval Innkeeper.

1393 A law was introduced compelling London innkeepers to display a sign. Florence North, a Chelsea brewer, was 'presented' for not having a sign at her inn. This law was the first indication that it was compulsory for a brewer to notify the ale-conner in this manner; in other trades the hanging of a sign was optional.

1400 First record of beer (made with hops) being imported: it came in through Winchelsea Harbour and was not for sale, but for Dutch merchants working in England.

1406 'Mystery' of Free Brewers was set up: formally constituted by Royal Ordinance as a specific form of tradesman, known as 'Free Brewers within the City', it had a Master, two wardens and five other members. They regulated the 'mystery of Brewing' and were responsible for seeing only good brews were available and that only the legal price was charged.

1422 30 July: the Master of the Free Brewers, together with 12 other members, was ordered to attend at the Guildhall by Sir Richard Whittington, the Lord Mayor of London, to answer complaints of overcharging for their beer. Whittington alleged that they had cornered the market in malt by buying up the barley in advance, and had made an excess profit selling the barley to individual brewers. They were fined £20, which they refused to pay. They were kept locked up in the Chamberlain's office until they paid, or could find bail. There were many other conflicts between the brewers and the 'Man with the cat'.

1423 Robert Chicheley, Lord Mayor of London, ordered that retailers of ale should sell it in their houses, 'in pots of pewtre, sealed [stamped] and open'; that whoever carried ale to the buyer should hold the pot in one hand and a cup in the other; and that all who had pots unsealed should be fined.

1428 First record of hops being successfully grown in England.

1437 22 February: Henry VI formally granted a Charter to brewers of the City of London, who were given a monopoly of the brewing trade throughout the country for ever.

1446 First mention of the Craft of Hostelers; possibly this was its foundation date.

1468 A Coat of Arms was granted to the Brewers' Society, which adopted St Mary and St Thomas the Martyr (Thomas a' Becket) as its patron saints. Thomas a' Becket's emblems were dropped when Henry VIII decreed him to be no longer a saint and ordered the Brewers' Company to change their arms.

The Ancient Arms.

1474 Brewers were ordered to regulate the price of ale according to the cost of a quarter of malt: the price ratio was ¼d per gallon to every shilling of the cost of a quarter the malt. Thus, when malt cost 2/– a quarter, a gallon of ale cost ½d, and so on.

Retailers were warned that 'Ale is not to be sold until it has been tested by the ale testers ... measures to be sized and sealed'.

1475 The Mystery of Bottlemakers merged with the Mystery of Horners. The bottlemakers had been recognized as a trade since 1373.

1488 Brewers in Canterbury were evading the regulations by which they were bound. By moving their address from 'within' to 'without' the town boundary they were putting themselves outside the local laws. Having moved, they were able to sell ale and beer to 'divers and many simple and evil disposed persons of the same citie, as well as to Scottes, Irish and other, which in no wise will apply themselves to labour or other lawful occupations but only they live upon sale and hucksterie of ale'. The authorities in Canterbury, however, countered those outside the boundaries by issuing a decree that no 'foreign' beer was to be sold in the city, and that brewers were to sell no ale, 'except to such as shall be of good disposition and conversation'. Such decrees were common throughout the country in towns of any size.

1492 The Red Lion Brewery, Smithfield, London E1, was established by John Marchant. The brewery, together with the Toby Jug trademark, was taken over by Charringtons in 1933.

1495 First licensing statute empowering JPs '... to take sureties of keepers of alehouses.

A Sixteenth-century Cooperage.

1501 The Mystery of Coopers was granted its Charter.

1509-47 Henry VIII zealously regulated the quality and price of ale, paying no attention to the rising prices of barley or the depreciation of the coinage.

1543 Beer exports were regulated by an Act which ordered that no vessel larger than a barrel be used for export purposes.

1547 The first mention of hops on the Statute Book. A decree was issued that all arable land should be dug up except 'land set aside for saffron and hops'.

1550 There were 26 brewers registered in the City of London. By the mid-17th century there were 199, with a further 675 in England and Wales.

A 16th-century brewery

Licensing systems of a sort came into being: curfew closing was brought in at 9pm in summer and 8pm in winter.

1552 Act of Parliament brought to an end the Court leets authority on licensed houses and placed it in the hands of the Justice of the Peace. Guidelines were laid down:

    a. to control the amount of drinking.

    b. to protect the public against monopolies which might be associated with the granting of licences.

Alehouse keepers and victuallers must provide

convenient lodging and good wholesome victuals to all such as upon honest occasions shall repair to their house. No gaming was allowed. No eating or drinking at the time of divine service, no flesh to be dressed or eaten during Lent.

1552–3 An Act, requiring tippling houses to be licensed, recognized the 'hurts and troubles caused by disorders in common ale houses and other houses called Tippling Houses'. The 1495 Act had given the magistrates power to suppress only: this Act gave them power to select so elevating the alehouse keeper to a person of privilege.

A regulation of Edward VI's reign prescribed that there were to be no more than 40 taverns (not alehouses) in London; Bristol, a minor port in those days, was to have 6; Cambridge, Canterbury, Chester, Exeter, Gloucester, Newcastle-on-Tyne, and Norwich had 4; Colchester, Hereford, Ipswich, Lincoln, Oxford, Salisbury, Shrewsbury, Southampton, Westminster, Winchester, and Worcester had 3. Not more than 2 upon average were allowed in each parish. Members of the Vintners' Company were exempt. The first time that a drunkard could be imprisoned.

1555 The export of beer was prohibited to conserve supplies of wheat and other corn for home requirements.

1558–1603 Records show that the ale Queen Elizabeth drank for breakfast was 'so strong there was no man durst touch it'. A much stronger ale, in both cask and bottle for home and export, came into use and made English ale famous throughout Europe. This greatly enhanced the status of the brewers. The Queen issued regulations by the score in defence of ale.

1559 First order banning gambling in pubs was issued by the Manchester Court Leet.

1568 First record of bottled beer: Dr Alexander Nowell, Dean of St Paul's Cathedral, who was partial to his home-brewed beer, put some in a bottle when he went fishing; placing the bottle on the bank he forgot to drink the contents. Some days later he remembered this and returned to collect it. He found the ale in perfect condition, but the cork came away with a loud bang.

1577 Ale was compared with beer and was described contemptuously as 'thick and fulsome, and no longer popular except with a few'.

Hops had become a 'necessity' in brewing; beer was the popular national drink.

First full census of alehouses, inns and pubs was taken. Covering England and Wales it showed 14,202 alehouses, 1,631 inns, 329 taverns and 3,597 which were not categorized, making 19,759 'pubs' or 1 for every 187 people. A financial levy was imposed on these Houses to repair Dover Harbour.

Manchester Court Leet issued a decree: 'In consideration whereof we order whomsoever shall hereafter offende in surffringe any unlawful games or mysorders in their houses, gardens or backsydes, not only that they do suffer the same mysorders but that they comytte ye same shall forfeyte to ye Lord for every tyme of offendinge 6/8d.' A further decree ordered that drinkers found on the streets or in alehouses should be punished 'all nighte in the Donngeon and moreover paie presently when they be released vid. to the constables to be given to the pore'.

1579 Elizabeth I ordered the brewers in Westminster to desist from using sea coal while she was in residence there. One brewer, John Platt, was imprisoned for disregarding this order.

1580 Representations were made to Queen Elizabeth to try to stop the proposed duty of 1d on each barrel of beer brewed, which would go a long way to solving the Exchequer's financial problems. The brewers threatened 'an immediate cessation of brewing' (surely the first strike planned in the brewing industry) leaving the City without beer.

The plan was dropped, being reintroduced without success in 1586, finally succeeding in 1643.

1583 The Ordinance of Vintners reveals that quart, pint, and half-pint pots marked to show their capacity were compulsory.

1587 The Privy Council issued a series of orders to magistrates over the next 90 years requiring them to suppress unnecessary alehouses in districts and towns where the needs of the inhabitants were more than fully met by the number then operating.

The City of London Brewery was founded by the Campion family at the Hour Glass Brewery, Upper Thames Street, London EC1. It was burned down during the Great Fire in 1666, but is commemorated in the name of Campion Lane.

1591 Brewers complained to Queen Elizabeth about competition from brandy and spirits, which (according to Camden) were introduced by English soldiers returning from fighting in the Low Countries.

A report by the Queen's Council told the Government that there were so many alehouses in Cheshire and Lancashire that on a Sunday the churches were almost deserted except for the curate and his cleric and that indulgence in alcohol was prevalent.

1600 The East India Company's first expedition sailed to the East in three ships with 150 barrels of beer to keep the crew happy. This shipment stood up well to the sea trip and led to experiments in shipping beer to the troops for the first time.

1603 James I decreed that all inkeepers, under pain of fine and imprisonment in default, were to sell 1 quarter of the best beer for 1d and 2 quarts of small beer for the same price. The fine for those who did not was 20/–, which was to be given for the relief of the poor of the parish.

1604 James I 'By the laws and statues of this our Realm' ordered that:

1 'The keeping of alehouses and victualling houses is none of those trades which is free and lawful for any subject to set up and exercise; but inhibited to all save such as are thereto licensed – Whereas the ancient, true and principle use of wine, alehouse and victualling house was for the receipt, relief and lodging of wayfaring people travelling from place to place and for the supply of the wants of such people as are not able to make their provision of victuals and not meant for entertainment or harbouring of lewd and idle people to spend and consume their money and time in lewd and drunken manner; it is enacted that only travellers, and travellers' friends, and labourers for one hour at dinner time, or lodgers, can receive entertainment under penalty.'

2 'To restrain the inordinate haunting and tippling in inns, alehouses and other victualling houses ... the principal use of such places being for the relief of the wayfaring men and women, and to fulfil the requirements of those unable to store victuals in large quantities, nor

for the entertainment and harbouring of lewd
and idle people to spend and consume their
money and time in lewd and drunken manner.'

A further requirement was that parish constables
were required to inspect alehouses to ensure that
they were conducted properly. Owners that
allowed their customers to stay too long were fined
10/–, the money to be given to the poor of the
parish.

A tavern in Stuart times

1606 James I's Court had moved to Oxford the
previous year to avoid the plague in London. The
drunkenness of the Court was scandalizing the
Oxford townspeople. Those who stayed at an inn
for more than an hour at dinnertime, unless their
occupation or employment compelled them to
lodge at such a place, were to be fined 3/4d and
those who were actually drunk had to pay 5/–.
Non-payment would entail 4 or 6 hours in the stocks
respectively. A person drinking in a retail establishment in his own area was to be fined 3/4d or a
period in the stocks. Further occurrences of the
same offence incurred increased penalties. (6
hours in the stocks gave the offender ample time
in which to sober up).

1607 In an attempt to repress the odious and loathesome sin of drunkenness, a brewer would be fined 6/8d for delivering a barrel to any unlicensed tap-house.

The first shipment of beer for the American settlers left in the winter under Captain Newport: most of the substantial consignment was drunk by the sailors on the voyage!

1609 The Governor of Virginia sent a request for 2 brewers to be shipped out. This was a low-priority colony and the request was ignored; contrary to British custom, the settlers had to drink water.

1613 William Truman registered as a brewer at St Giles Without, Cripplegate. The first member of this famous brewing family to enter the trade. By 1760 the brewery produced 60,140 barrels of porter, and was the 3rd largest supplier in London at that time. By 1815, 272,162 barrels of porter were brewed. By 1840 the brewery was the 2nd largest in London; 263,235 barrels of porter were brewed, less than in 1815, but more breweries were brewing. None of the old Brick Lane brewery remains, but brewing still continues on the site.

1617 Licences were required if croquet and bowls were to be played at taverns; both games were being encouraged by the publicans of the day.

1618 Sir Walter Raleigh 'drank a cool tankard and smoked a soothing pipe of tobacco' before going to the scaffold.

Until this time inns had not been required to have a licence. Sir Giles Mompesson was granted a patent allowing him to licence inns and to retain half the licence fees. It is said that he gravely abused his powers, granting licences to alehouses that had been closed by the Justices on the grounds of disorderly conduct. Out of the 60 premises that he licensed in Hampshire, 17 had been previously closed down. In only 4 years he granted a total of 12,400 licences.

1621 Sir Giles Mompesson was impeached for abusing his powers. He claimed 'It was not profit that tied me to it but hope of reformation' to which an MP retorted 'The pretence of the patent was reformation, whereas, it was made defamation'. The King exiled Mompesson, and the licences he granted were abolished. The House of Lords resolved that 26 March should be a 'sermon' day for ever in memory of the punishment the King imposed on Mompesson.

1625 Charles I decreed that the citizens of London might hang signs in the streets and on poles so that their shop could be more easily found. This was carried to such lengths that a traveller in London wrote

> I'm amazed at the signs,
> As I pass through the town;
> To see the odd mixture
> A Magpie and Crown,
> The Razor and Heen [hen]
> The Leg and Seven Stars,
> The Axe and the Bottle . . .

There was no restriction on the size and publicans tried to outdo each other by erecting enormous signs.

1626 The authority of the Brewers' Company was dwindling; only 6 brewers and a few home-brewers out of many hundreds in the whole country were members. The Company asked the City Fathers to decree that no one within the City of London limits should be permitted to brew unless he was a member of the Brewers' Company. The breweries were fast becoming large family businesses and their owners were improving their own social standing.

> 'Men of good rank and place, and much command
> Who have, by sodden water, purchased land.'

1627 An Act was passed that added to the penalties for drunkenness by allowing the habitual drunkard to be sentenced to a public whipping.

1629 The *Arbella* carrying settlers, under John Wintrop, and 42 tons (almost 10,000 gallons) of beer landed at Plymouth, Massachusetts. Soon after their arrival the settlers founded the first brewery in North America. They received malt from England but, if the shipments failed to arrive, they used local barley. (The Puritans drank beer as a substitute for fresh vegetables.)

1630 The Royal Oak Brewery, Surrey Street, Croydon, was founded.

1634 The Governor of Massachusetts Bay enacted the first drink-related law in the American Colonies setting the price of beer at 1d per quart.

1635 The vintners obtained the right to sell beer, tobacco and food in their taverns; previously they had only sold wine. It was said that they paid the King £6000 for the privilege. The room in which wine was served was usually situated above the area in which beer was sold.

> 'A Tavern is a degress, a pair of stairs above an Alehouse, where men drink with more credit and apology ... It is a broacher of more news than hogsheads, and more jests than news. Men come here to make merry, but indeed make a noise, and their music above is answered with the clinking below.'   John Earle, 17th century

A Proclamation was issued ordering a considerable reduction in the number of Brewers, prohibiting home-brew Houses in towns. All requirements were to be purchased through the common Brewer whose prices were rigidly controlled. Punishment was to be meted out through the infamous Star Chamber. The Lyme Regis local authority decreed 'No innkeeper or Tippler that might conveniently be served by any common Brewer, admitted or to be admitted in the town of Lyme, was to brew in their houses, but to buy of the common Brewers, and such drink only, and of such reasonable size as should be fit for travellers and passengers, and such as the Mayor and his Brethren should set down as fit and of such a price'.

4 March: first Licensing Laws in the American Colonies. An 'ordinaire' keeper was to be licensed. (Taverns were called ordinaires.)

The Royal Postal Service was opened to the public, innkeepers being the postmasters.

1637 Drunkenness in the American Colonies had become so serious that more stringent decrees were issued. Only common Brewers were to brew beer, all other brewing (home-brew mainly) was prohibited.

Mother Louse, alewife, 1673-8

1639 Home-brewing restrictions were lifted in the American Colonies. The breweries were unable to produce enough beer and heavy drinking of spirits was filling the gap, with associated drunkenness.

There were 24 alehouses in Covent Garden alone.

1643 On 16 May Parliament established the first excise duty on beer at 2/– a barrel for beer brewed at a brewhouse and 6d a barrel for beer brewed at a private house for the household's own consumption. The Royalists followed suit establishing excise duty in Oxford (their headquarters). Both parties declared that the tax would last only for the duration of the war. However, it continued throughout the Commonwealth period and subsequently reverted to the Crown, where it remained until 1757. The duty was not finally abolished until the 1830 Beer Act was passed. A distinction was made, however, between weak and strong beer.

1648 The shortage of small coins led to copper and brass tokens being issued by traders, including publicans. These tokens were legal tender supplementing the supply of farthings, halfpennies and, to a lesser extent, pennies. The obverse of the token bore the name of the establishment issuing it and the reverse bore the value. They were withdrawn in 1672. (It is from these tokens that the phrase 'brass farthing' originates.)

*c***1650** Mansell designed the first English beer glasses, a type of cylindrical beaker which was large and heavy. Some had an extra piece of glass in the bottom to strengthen them.

Tax on a barrel of strong beer was 2/6d. Importation of spirits was forbidden, but on payment of small duties anyone could distil and retail spirits made from English-grown corn. This caused an increase in the amount of spirits people drank.

1655 The largest inn-sign ever erected was built by James Peck, a Norfolk merchant, at the White Hart, Scoale, and was described by Sir Thomas Browne in 1663: 'I came to Scoale where there is a very handsome inne, and the noblest signpost in England about and upon which was carved a great many stories as of Charon and Cerberus, Actaeon and Diana, and many others; the signe itself is a White Hart, which hanges down carved in a stately wreath.'

1657 An Act was passed authorizing Excise Officers to enter and search the premises of persons suspected of brewing, and to seize any wort or beer that was not duly declared. At the end of each week the brewer was required to attend at the Revenue Office and declare the amount of beer and ale he had produced.

The first coaching route from Chester to London was established.

1658 5 October: first beer was brewed at the Cape, South Africa, from locally-grown barley.

1660–85 Charles II increased the tax on beer to $\frac{1}{2}$d on beer selling at more than 6/– a barrel and to 3d on small beer costing less than 6/– a barrel, in order to raise funds for restoring order after the Civil War.

1660 Parliament was petitioned (unsuccessfully) by the Brewers' Company in London and Westminster for freedom from the 'illegal and intolerable' burden of excise, which they described at 'burdonsome to the poor to whom ale and beer, next to bread, are the chief stay – and ruinous to us'.

1661 A duty on spirits was first imposed at 11/8¼d per gallon in England, 6/2d in Scotland, and 5/7d in Ireland. The beer tax had caused people to turn to gin drinking (as much from cussedness in refusing to pay tax as from pleasure). It was the start of the greatest and most harmful period of drunkenness in British history – a social disaster of horrible proportions.

1662 Dr Robert Vilaine gave control of the brewery on Exe Island, Exeter, to his nephew Simon Snow, leaving the brewhouse to Exeter City Council for ever, to be managed for the public good of the city. It has had many owners over the years, eventually being acquired by Whitbreads.

1663 Turnpike Act passed and the start of toll houses, many of which became pubs; the toll keeper eked out his meagre pay by selling beer.

1666 Henry Campion's Brewery was rebuilt following the Great Fire, at Thames-side in the City of London. By 1744 Sir William Calvert, one-time Lord Mayor of London, had become the owner and in 1760 it was the 4th largest brewery in London, brewing 63,500 barrels annually.

1667 An Act was passed restricting overhanging signs: 'No signboard shall hang across, but the sign shall be fixed against the balconies, or some convenient part of the side of the house.'

1669 The Lancaster Brewery of Yates and Jackson was built at Brock Street, Lancaster. An independent brewery, it is still in production with over 40 tied Houses.

Hythe Brewery (now owned by Mackeson) was founded by James Pashley.

1670 The Guinness Brewery site in Dublin was obtained by Giles Mee; in order to start brewing he purchased, from the municipal corporation, certain water rights on ground called The Pipes in the Parish of St James.

1673 A petition against imported beverages was presented to Parliament. It requested that brandy, coffee, rum, tea, and chocolate be prohibited 'for these greatly hinder the consumption of barley, malt and wheat, the product of our Land'.

1676 The first mention of beer being bottled in quantity. George Cross, a brewer at Woburn, supplied beer to the Russell family (the Dukes of Bedford). $10\frac{1}{2}$ barrels (some 1,500 quarts) were purchased to bottle 'for my Lord's drinking'.

1680 The Horndean Brewery, Hants, was in existence in a wooden structure at the Ship and Bell. It was destroyed by fire in 1869, when the present brewery was built. A family brewery with just under 100 Houses, it does not sell to the Free Trade.

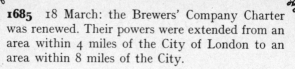

1685 18 March: the Brewers' Company Charter was renewed. Their powers were extended from an area within 4 miles of the City of London to an area within 8 miles of the City.

1689 The duty on beer was increased by 50% to 2/9d a barrel.

1690 An Act was passed (as a result of pressure started in 1673) giving any Englishman the right to distil and retail spirit produced from English corn (so decreasing the import of brandy). The effect was that gin distilling increased rapidly, especially in London.

1692 The tax on beer was increased to nearly 5/– a barrel and consumption fell rapidly, which further increased gin drinking. The consumption of beer in London dropped from 2,088,000 barrels in 1690 to 1,523,000 barrels in 1693.

Skidmore's Bury Lane Brewery was founded in the High Street, Rickmansworth.

1694 An Act further restraining the sale of ale was passed.

1696 Hampstead Brewery, North London, was founded.

1697 A duty was imposed on malt for the first time.

1700 Prestonpans Brewery, Scotland, was in being, now a subsidiary of United Caledonian Breweries.

1704 Garratt & Co's Brewery was founded in Portsmouth, but is probably much older having been founded as a brewery on the instructions of Henry VII (250 years earlier) to supply sailors based in Portsmouth.

1706 The Act of Union was passed. The Government imposed a tax on malt throughout the Union.

1707 Wilson and three others founded a brewery (later to become Allsopp and Sons) at Burton-on-Trent on a site of over 50 acres. (The official date is given as 1730.)

Oh well I love the pewter
With ale of Allsopp in it!
My thirst becomes acuter –
I quaff it in a minute.
But now I mean to mention
A liquid that surpasses
Great Allsopp's chief invention –
And that's the nectar of the lasses.

Champagne that's wont to sparkle
Is very pretty tipple,
And port that's patriarchal
Will jollify a cripple;
But far the rarest liquor
To cream into your glasses,
And make your blood run quicker,
Is the kisses of the lasses.

The Very Best Tipple by Old Thirsty

1710 Archibald Campbell founded the Argyll Brewery in Edinburgh.

Harvesting the hops in the 17th century

1711 A duty was imposed on hops for the first time and a similar duty was levied on malt (repealed in 1862). This further encouraged the distillers of spirits, especially gin.

[31]

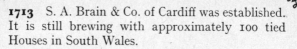

1713 S. A. Brain & Co. of Cardiff was established. It is still brewing with approximately 100 tied Houses in South Wales.

1715 Beamish & Crawford, South Main Street, Cork, was founded by Edward Allan. By 1809 it was the largest brewery in Ireland.

1719 Belhaven Brewery started brewing in Dunbar, Scotland. When Boswell stopped at Dunbar he had some beer and reported that it was 'the best small beer I ever had'. The Emperor of Austria said of Belhaven beer: 'It is the Burgundy of Scotland. Bavaria cannot produce the like.'

Stone Brewery ales were produced by a monk until the Joule family took over in 1785. The brewery was closed in 1974. Joules bitter is now brewed at Burton-on-Trent.

1720 First mention of a 'bottle scrue' (corkscrew).

Norwich's King Street Old Brewery was founded – now owned by Watneys.

1722 A blend of various beers was prepared by Harwood at the Bell brewhouse, Shoreditch, and was sold as 'entire' (later known as porter). It was first sold in the Blue Last, Great Eastern Street, Shoreditch; a pub still stands on this site.

1723 Cobbold & Co Brewery was founded at Harwich.

1725 28 August: Scottish Brewers of Edinburgh decided to stop brewing. The Scots took to drinking whisky.

1729 The 1552 Act, which gave any two magistrates power to grant a licence at any time of the year, was revoked, and the Brewster Sessions were instituted. Licences could only be granted at a General Sessions of the Justices of that division.

First Gin Act, when duty of 5/– a gallon imposed on gin and other compounded spirits.

1730 Salter & Company's Brewery, Rickmansworth was founded by Samuel Salter. In 1841 another Salter made a bequest that a barrel of beer was to be supplied daily for the refreshment of parishioners and travellers. The barrel was placed outside in the yard each morning for people to help themselves but it had to be moved to the old malthouse entrance. After a few years, because of the nuisance caused by the crowds that gathered – up to 100 every morning, the practice was discontinued.

Isleworth Brewery, London was established.

The Old Brewery, Uxbridge was founded. It was acquired by Courage, Barclay Simonds with over 200 pubs in 1962.

1736 C. P. Christies' Hoddesdon Brewery, Herts, was founded. Recently it joined the Allied Group.

29 September: 2nd Gin Act: 'The drinking of spiritous liquors or strong waters has become very common, especially among the people of the lower and inferior rank, the constant and excessive use whereof tends greatly to the destruction of their health, rendering them unfit for useful labour and business, debauching their morals and making them perpetrate all manner of vices ...' All persons selling less than 2 gallons of spirits at a time were required to take out a licence costing; £50; a duty of £1 was imposed on every gallon sold; in addition duties were payable by distillers and by retailers, who had to keep a victualling house, and have no other business interests. There was a penalty of £100 for any person selling without a licence. Every conceivable type of evasion was practised and the consumption of gin in England and Wales almost doubled in a few years. Most taverns went into mourning by draping their signs with black velvet or added black to their names. Thus there are now pubs called the Black Dog, Black Swan, etc.

In spite of the £100 penalty for selling without a licence, 12,000 persons had been prosecuted by 1738. In order to help in detection the Act provided for 'one moiety of the fines, penalties and forfeitures to be paid to his Majesty and successors, the other to the person who shall inform on anyone for the same'. Informers earned easy money instituting prosecutions!

1739 Williamson, Bow Lane, Cheapside, (now the Mansion House) became a tavern. Previously the official residence of the Lord Mayor of London; said to be the exact Centre of the City of London. William III and Mary dined there and presented the iron gates with their coat of arms in appreciation.

Joseph and Ephraim Thwaites founded a brewery in Dublin, in spite of there being 70 other breweries operating in the city.

1740 Court Street Brewery, Faversham, Kent, was founded.

James Aitkin, Newmarket Street, Falkirk, was established. It ceased brewing under United Caledonian Breweries in 1963.

1742 Samuel Whitbread, the 7th of 8 children, with £2000 capital and a partner, Shewell, set up a brewery on 11 December in Golden Lane, Old Street, City. By 1746 they had 13 tied Houses. In 1750 they moved to Chiswell Street, and by 1756 had 24 tied Houses. In 1760 they were producing 63,408 barrels of porter annually, and were the 2nd largest brewery in London. By 1786 they were producing 150,280 barrels of beer annually. By 1800 Whitbreads owned 80 tied Houses. A vat 65ft in diameter, 25ft high, and with 56 hoops (each weighing up to 3 tons), which held the contents of 20,000 barrels, took 4 years to build. Alas! the brewery has recently been demolished.

The Devenish Brewery was founded at Weymouth, Dorset, although the family name has only been used since 1824. Brewing has taken place here since the 13th century.

1743 The Gin Act of 1736 was repealed. The licence fee was reduced to £1 (from £50) and the duty of £1 per gallon on beer was abolished.

A survey showed that out of a total of 94,968 Houses in London, 15,288 sold drink for consumption on the premises. The population was 725,903, (1 licensed House for every 47 inhabitants!) The breakdown showed 5,975 ale-houses, 654 inns and taverns, and 8,659 spirit bars.

1744 Licences were only to be granted to keepers of public houses and for one House only, so preventing the growth of a chain of Houses, under dubious management. Licence holders were not to be grocers, chandlers, or distillers.

Worthington & Co was founded at Burton-on-Trent; it merged with Bass in 1927.

1745 Marston's Dolphin Brewery was established in Poole – now owned by Whitbreads.

Griffin Hock Brewery, Chiswick, W. London, was founded. It is now owned by Fuller, Smith and Turner with over 100 tied Houses.

1746 The Glass Excise Act taxed glass by weight, which led to the introduction of lighter, more elegant, and highly decorated glasses.

1749 The Leith Brewery, Edinburgh, was founded by William Younger, who appears as Father William in their trademark. Later it moved to Holyrood Abbey, near the present site. In 1802 they purchased vaults on South London's riverside, and began shipping beer by sea.

1750 The Emsworth Brewery in South Street, Hants, was established.

The Ballinghall Park, Pleasure Brewery, Dundee, was founded.

1751 An Act was passed preventing distillers from selling retail, or to unlicensed publicans. It decreed that debts for drink could not be recovered through the courts; and raised the duty on spirits. 'This Act really did reduce the excessive spirit drinking: it was the turning point in the social history of London.'

'While the period of cheap gin lasted (1720–1750) it had done much to reduce the population of the capital. In the country at large, its ravages had been severe, but ale had held its own better in the village than in the town.' G. M. Trevelyan, *English Social History*.

The Cannon Brewery, St John Street, Clerkenwell, London EC1, was established. The site is now the London HQ of Allied.

1752 First Act requiring a special licence for music and dancing in inns.

1753 Annual licences became a statutory requirement, and were issued only at Brewster Sessions. Justices were given greater powers of control. The

licensee had to produce sureties for his good be-
haviour and registers were introduced.

1754 The Penrith Brewery, Westmorland, was
founded.

Hartleys Brewery, Ulverston, was founded. It is
still an independent brewery with 80 tied Houses.

Home brewhouse vat

1756 A public brewery was built in Meadow Lane,
Leeds. Later it became the Leeds and Wakefield
Melbourne Brewery, which was acquired, with 245
pubs, by Joshua Tetley in May 1960 for £3,500,000.
Tetley merged with Ind Coope and Ansells to form
Allied Breweries in 1961.

1757 Robert Westfield and Joseph Moss founded
the Anchor Brewery of Charrington & Co at
Bethnal Green in the East End of London. John
Charrington, a vicar's son, joined the firm in 1766
and it traded as Charrington & Moss until he
obtained sole control in 1783. It is only recently
that the family have left the board of Bass Charrington. It ceased brewing in London in 1974.

Mercer Street Brewery, London, WC2, was sold to
Meux and Mungo Murray for £15,000. In 1760
10,012 barrels of porter were brewed making the
brewery the 10th largest in London. In 1795 the
brewery (by then in Liquorpond Street) had
Britain's largest vat: 22ft high, it held 20,000 barrels
of beer (nearly ¾ million gallons). On 17 October
1814 this vat burst its hoops; in the flood of porter
8 people died, some drowned in the beer, one died of

[37]

drunkenness from the unexpected free beer and others were buried in buildings demolished by the flood. By 1815, 282,104 barrels of porter were being brewed annually; the brewery was the 2nd largest in London.

The Crown Steam Brewery, Ripon, Yorks, was established.

1759 Arthur Guinness started brewing in Dublin, having bought the lease of the 4-acre site from Mark Rainsford, a brewer. The annual rent was £45.

1760 Lady Parsons owned a brewery in London that produced 34,098 barrels of porter.

1761 Beer duty was raised by 3/– a barrel, the first rise for 50 years. This long period of stability has not been equalled since.

Calvert and Seward brewed 63,500 barrels of beer in London; they were the largest London brewers at that time. Now part of the Bass empire.

1762 Greenall Whitley's Warrington Brewery, Lancs, was founded by Thomas Greenall. It is now the largest private brewing company in Britain.

1763 Henry Thrale (son of Ralph Thrale, MP for Southwark) worked in Southwark Brewery for 6/– a week. Eleven years later he was wealthy enough to purchase the brewery for £30,000 having married Hester Lynch. Their marriage of convenience was breaking up when Samuel Johnson met the couple, became enamoured of Mrs Thrale 'his provider and conductress'. By 1760 30,740 barrels of porter were brewed annually, making the brewery the 7th largest in London. In 1764 Dr Johnson took over the running of the brewery (Thrale had died in 1759). He adopted modern methods and paid off some £13,000 in debts that Thrale had incurred: 'The Brewery must be the scene of action, not the subject of speculation.' John Perkins, a Quaker, was appointed manager. On 31 May 1781, the brewery was auctioned: 'We are not here to sell a parcel of boilers and vats, but the potential of growing rich beyond the dream of avarice.' Robert Barclay from the American Colonies bought the brewery for £135,000 with Silvanus Bevan as partner and John Perkins as manager and technical advisor. All four were Quakers. By 1785 the full purchase price was paid and Barclay Perkins was formed.

The Alton Brewery, Hants, was established by James Baverstock.

1764 An Act was passed ordering the removal of dangerous, projecting inn signs. The old Act of 1667 seems to have lapsed, as this one no longer stipulated that they should be on the wall of the house.

A Frenchman writing earlier in the 18th century described inn signs thus: 'At London they are commonly very large, and jut out so far, that in some narrow streets they touch each other; nay, and run across quite to the other side. They are generally adorned with carving and gilding; and there are several that, with the branches of iron that support them, cost about a hundred guineas . . . Out of London, and particularly in villages the Signs are suspended in the middle of a great wooden portal, which may be looked upon as a kind of triumphal arch to the honour of Bacchus.'

1765 2 Justices of Corfe Castle were committed to prison for 1 month and fined £50 each for refusing to grant a licence to an innkeeper because he had voted in the Parliamentary Election for a candidate they opposed.

The Anchor Brewery, Hull, was established. It is now trading as North Country Breweries.

1767 The Oakhill Brewery, Somerset, was founded – famous for its 'invalid stout'.

Buckley's Brewery, Llanelli, South Wales, was founded. It is still brewing with 180 tied Houses in South Wales.

1768 Randall's Channel Island Brewery was founded. A private company, it is still brewing.

*c***1770** George III (incognito) attending a cockfight in Clerkenwell had gambled all his money, and was unable to hire a cab. He went into the first pub he came across, the Castle, in Cow Cross Street, Farringdon, and asked the landlord if he could pledge his gold watch for a sovereign. The landlord said that he didn't have a Pawnbroker's Licence but since the surety was so good, if he returned the next day, he would be glad to return the watch without interest. The next day an Equerry returned the sovereign together with a Pawnbroker's Licence (as a gift). It was only then that the landlord realized whom he had befriended, and to this day The Castle is the only public house with a Pawnbroker's Licence.

1770 Barclay Perkins first brewed their famous Russian Stout for the Czar of Russia and his Court. It became popular in the Baltic and in England during the porter-drinking days and is still brewed.

1771 F. Mitchell founded Mitchell's Brewery, Chard. It is now a Bass Charrington depot.

The Quay Brewery, Ely, Cambs, was established.

1772 The Castle Bellingham Brewery was founded in Eire; in 1959 it was acquired by Guinness.

A Mug House

1773 The brewing industry in Ireland had declined to such an extent that the cost of the collection of the Malt Tax was not covered by the amount collected! The imports of porter, mainly from Georges at Bristol and through Liverpool, increased from 28,935 barrels to 56,675 barrels in 3 years. This was due to the tax on imported beer being a fraction of 1/– against a tax of nearly 5/6d a barrel on locally-brewed beer, which placed the local brewers at a hopeless disadvantage.

1774 Broad Street Brewery, Reading, was founded by William Blackall Simonds. In 1813 the brewery made a contract with the newly-opened Royal Military College, Camberley, which was the start of Simonds' association with the Army, which they supplied with beer throughout the world. Mr F. A. Simonds was Chairman to the Brewers' Society 'Beer for the Troops Committee' in both world wars. In 1960 the brewery amalgamated with others forming Courage, Barclay Simonds, but in 1970 reverted to Courage. In 1789 the brewery

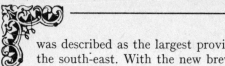

was described as the largest provincial brewery in the south-east. With the new brewery under construction on the M4, it may become that again.

Allsopp & Son shipped 600 hogsheads at a time from Burton-on-Trent to St Petersburg. Catherine the Great, who had usurped the throne from her husband, was still drinking ale supplied by Allsopps. However, she was persuaded by her Minister, Prince Potemkin, to place a particularly prohibitive import duty on this beverage; but Allsopps soon found markets in the Polish provinces, where it became a great favourite, especially among the nobility.

1775 The Basingstoke Brewery, Hants, was founded.

The Milton Brewery, Blandford, Dorset, was founded by Robert Fookes. In 1950 it was acquired with 12 Houses by J. W. Groves of Weymouth, (which later amalagamated with Devenish). The original building is now a Brewery and Farm Museum, which is run by a grandson of the founder. Some of the author's collection of pub regalia and inn signs may be seen here.

1777 William Bass sold his transport business (to Mr Pickford) and started brewing in Burton.

Hall & Woodhouse opened their brewery in Anstey, Dorset.

1778 Archibald C. Younger founded the Edinburgh Brewery which 'brewed so powerful a beer, it almost glued the lips together'. In 1821 his brewery amalgamated with that of William Younger.

1779 The Admiralty ordered all naval ships on foreign service to carry dehydrated malt (invented by Jackson) as a remedy for scurvy, and to make available badly-needed space, which had previously been occupied by barrels of beer. Supplemented by the rum issue (grog), it was finally dropped when concentrated lime juice was used to combat scurvy. This gave rise to the American term 'limey' so amazed were they to see the British drinking lime juice. Had the War of Independence been a few years earlier, they might have referred to us as 'hoppies'.

1780 In order to finance the War of American Independence, Lord North increased the duty on malt and hops. The private brewer and the farmer were the worst hit, to the advantage of the common brewer. Brewers gradually reduced the strength of porter in an effort to keep prices stable, and to compete with the new paler beers to which the public was slowly turning.

Cheapside Brewery, Liverpool, was founded.

Cheltenham Original Brewery was established, later becoming West Country Breweries. Recently acquired by Whitbreads.

1782 A third beer was added for duty purposes so there were strong, table, and small beers. This only led to more confusion and arguments. The methods used for gauging the strength of the wort were crude, e.g. inserting a finger in the liquid and licking it.

1783 7 November: the last execution to be carried out at Tyburn took place. Now the site of Marble Arch, this was where the Gentlemen of the Road were hanged in style. On his final journey from Newgate gaol to Tyburn every highwayman was allowed to stop at least twice, and drink his fill. The first stop was usually the George and Blue Boar, High Holborn, where a glass of wine was taken (the commoner type of criminal drank a bowl of ale).

1784 Pitt increased the brewing licence fee to £1 11s minimum for up to 1000 barrels.

The first Royal Mail service was introduced having coaching houses as post offices.

1785 Thomas Tipper founded the Newhaven Brewery, Sussex. His epitaph is in St Michael's Churchyard:

> Reader with kind regard this grave survey,
> Nor heedless pass where Tipper's ashes lay,
> Honest he was, ingenious, blunt and kind
> And dared do, what few dare do, speak his mind.
> Philosophy and history he knew
> Was versed in physicke and surgery too;
> The beer old stingo he both brewed and sold.
> He played through life a varied part,
> And knew immortal Hubibras by heart,
> Reader in truth such was the man,
> Be better, wiser, laugh more if you can.

A glass especially designed for the Newhaven Tipper can be seen at the Cinque Ports pub, Seaford.

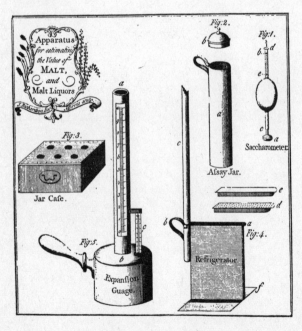

The Saccharometer invented by Benjamin Baverstock; its introduction into brewing caused a minor upheaval, but was in everyday use by 1816.

1786 Forth Brewery, Alloa, was established by Robert Knox. In 1954 it became a distillery.

1787 A Royal Proclamation against vice and immorality was sent to all Magistrates. There was to be a general tightening up of the issuing and renewing of licences.

Tokens were re-introduced because of the shortage of small change; they were withdrawn in 1797.

George III and Queen Charlotte visited Whitbreads Brewery to inspect the newly-installed steam engine, which was the wonder of London. Dr John Wolcot ('Peter Pinder') celebrated the occasion:

> The monarch heard of Whitbread's fame;
> Quoth he unto the Queen 'My dear, my dear,
> Whitbread hath got a marvellous great name,
> Clearly, we must, must, must see Whitbread's
> brew.'

and about Whitbread's preparations for the visit:

> He gave his maids new aprons, gowns and
> smocks;
> And lo! two hundred pounds were spent on
> frocks

and the inspection by the King:

> And now his curious Majesty did stoop
> To count the nails on every hoop;
> And lo! no single thing came in his way,
> That full of deep research, he did not say
> 'What's this, he, he? What's that? What's
> This? What's that?'
> So quick the words too when he deigned to
> speak
> As if each syllable would break its neck.

and to taste the beer:

> 'Not to forget to take of beer the cask
> The brewer offered me, away.'

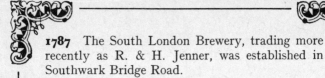

1787 The South London Brewery, trading more recently as R. & H. Jenner, was established in Southwark Bridge Road.

Wilderspool Brewery, Warrington, Lancs, was founded.

1788 Alton & Co's Warwick Brewery, 15 Wardweek, Derby, was established.

Boddington Brewery was founded. It has survived with approximately 280 pubs.

Bristol Brewery was established by Isaac Hobhouse, whose descendants are still associated with Courage Western; it originated in 1730 as George's.

1790 Macclesfield Brewery, Cheshire, was established.

Bridge Wharf Brewery, Lewes, Sussex, was founded. A family brewery still brewing with 24 tied Houses and also supplying 26 Beard Tied Houses.

James Calder & Co's Shore Brewery, Alloa, was founded. Now a subsidiary of Bass Charrington.

Elgood & Sons, Wisbech, Cambridge, was built. In 1877 it was purchased by John Elgood and still exists with 70 tied Houses.

1791 Edward Allen founded the Cork Porter Brewery, Ireland.

1792 Workington Brewery was founded. In keeping with the John Peel country in which it is situated, it has a huntsman trademark. An independent brewery, it has over 100 pubs.

Old Hornchurch Brewery, Hornchurch, Essex, was in existence.

Pitt introduced the first Reform Bill to curb drunkenness.

1795 Sale of Beer Act: Any person convicted for

the second time of selling without a licence would be barred from holding any further licence for the retailing of spirits, beer, etc.

Swan Brewery, Oxford, was founded. It is now part of the Allied group.

Bentley & Shaw's Lockwood Brewery, Huddersfield, Yorks, was founded. It was acquired by Hammond's Bradford Brewery in 1944.

1796 An Act was passed compelling brewers to brew table beer as such. At that time beers from one brew and 'spargings' were mixed and sold as table beer.

Chipping Norton Brewery was founded.

Dorsetshire Brewery, Sherborne, Dorset, was established. Now a part of Bass Charrington.

Charles Ashby & Co, Church Street, Staines, Middx, was established. In 1929 it was acquired by Wheeler's Wycombe Brewery.

1798 Burford Brewery, Oxon, was founded. It was acquired with 9 pubs by Wadworths of Devizes.

1799 Dutton's Blackburn Brewery was founded by Thomas Dutton and his son William on land bought from the Vicar of Blackburn. It was taken over by Whitbreads in 1964.
'O! Be Joyful', the famous brew remains, but little else.

Greene King of Bury St Edmunds was founded. It is still independent with over 900 tied Houses, mainly in East Anglia.

1800 Beer money was introduced in the Army. A sum of 1d a day was paid to NCOs and soldiers on home service as a substitute for an issue of beer, etc. This was in addition to the daily rate of pay and continued until 1874, when it was consolidated into the rates of pay.

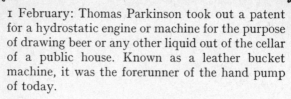

I February: Thomas Parkinson took out a patent for a hydrostatic engine or machine for the purpose of drawing beer or any other liquid out of the cellar of a public house. Known as a leather bucket machine, it was the forerunner of the hand pump of today.

1801 There were 49,000 full licences for a population of 8,893,000, in the only year a census of licensed premises was carried out in the 19th century.

1802 Richard Flower of Flower's Brewery published a radical pamphlet entitled 'Observation on the Malt Tax' in which he complained of the inequality of the tax on the brewer, the publican, and their customers.

> O! think ye, high rulers, ere time bears away,
> The labourers strength thro' the laws of our
>   day,
> How hard 'tis they took to replenish your store;
> O! tax not that liquor which cheers up the poor!

1804 A Stamp Act was introduced increasing the duty for a Publican's Licence to 2 guineas.

1807 Meux Horseshoe Brewery (off Tottenham Court Road) was the biggest producer of beer in London. Its main produce was porter.

1811 Tokens were re-introduced because of the general shortage of small change; they were withdrawn in 1817.

1813 The London Tavern, Windsor, Berks, is said to have been the first to be fitted with gas. George IV had gas lighting fitted in Windsor Castle and to celebrate this, the Chartered Gas Light and Coke Company held a celebration dinner under a splendid and attractive display of gas, both inside the pub and outside.

1816 The first record of Irish porter being exported: 10,000 barrels were sent to Liverpool.

There were 48,000 licensed alehouses of which 14,500 were brewery-owned. 10,800 were owner-occupied, and the other 22,700 were owned by purchasers or mortgagees. A House of Commons Committee reported that half the victualling houses in London were held by brewers. In Reading 61 of 68 pubs were brewery-owned.

Both parties in the Commons took exception to the powers invested in the magistrates regarding licensing laws and the Brewster Sessions; they considered it wrong that a publican could be deprived of his livelihood or a brewer of the value of his property. They thought that there should be as many alehouses or other kinds of retailer as could operate in any area. It took several more years for this to become law.

1821 William Cobbett the essayist wrote: 'Mr Ellman, an old man, and a large farmer in Sussex, has recently given in evidence before a Committee of the House of Commons this fact, that forty years ago there was not a labourer in his parish that did not brew his own beer, and that now there is not one that does it, except by chance the malt be given him.'

1823 Steps were taken to encourage cheaper beer, and the home-brewer was permitted to retail his product for consumption off his premises without a further licence.

1825 The Imperial Standard Gallon was introduced; it contained 277.27cu in against the 282cu in of the gallon it replaced.

1827–8 At Morely, Devon, the Magistrates granted licences to any man of reputable character who applied for one, so increasing the number of pubs from 60 to 110. They said that the brewer's trade should be as open as the trades of butcher and baker.

1828 Home Drummond Act, Scotland; power to regulate common inns, alehouses, and victualling houses in which ale, beer, spirits, wine and other excisable liquors were sold by retail under excise licence, was transferred to the Magistrates. This abolished the sureties, and heavier penalties were imposed for violations. The publican was forced to keep his premises closed on Sundays, Christmas Day, and Good Friday, except for travellers.

Brewster Sessions were defined: not more than 8 and not less than 4 meetings were to be held annually, allowing transfers to be carried out. No more financial bonds were required but simple restrictions were imposed. The publican was ordered:

1 not to keep his house open during Divine Service, nor on Sundays, Christmas Day, or Good Friday;
2 not to adulterate liquor;
3 to use only properly stamped measures; and
4 not to permit drunkenness, disorderly conduct, unlawful games, or gatherings of bad characters in his house.
5 right of appeal to quarter sessions against summary convictions or refusal by the Justices to grant transfer or renewal of the licence.

1830 Duke of Wellington's Beer House Act: to ease restrictions on the sale of beer and cider in England. Keepers of inns, alehouses, and victualling houses, to open at 4am and close 10pm and to close during Divine Service. Although its express object was to discourage the drinking of spirits, anyone who chose could open a 'pot-house'. The immediate effect of the Act was to encourage disorderly little pubs. The licence fee was 2 guineas for the general sale of beer and cider or, for cider only, 1 guinea. It was a blow to those who held a full Publican's Licence, but there were no objections raised as there was little sympathy for them.

In October the Beer Duty Act was repealed. Joulburn, Chancellor of the Exchequer in the Duke of Wellington's Cabinet, removed the tax on beer and cider, and threw open the retail sale of these beverages to combat the consumption of spirits, which had doubled between 1807 and 1827; while beer and ale licences had fallen, spirit licences had increased by 11,000. There was a considerable increase in Malt Duty.

The British and Foreign Temperance Society required its members to abstain from distilled liquors, but did not condemn fermented liquors such as beer, wine, and cider.

1834 The 1830 Beerhouse Act was amended. A distinction was drawn between 'on' and 'off' licences, reducing the fee for the 'off' to 1 guinea, increasing the 'on' to 3 guineas. The 'on' licence was granted only on production of a certificate of good character signed by 6 ratepayers. The full Publican's Licence was subject to the control of the Licensing Justices. 'The results of these measured were quite the opposite of those intended: those selling only beer were unable to make an honest living in competition with the publicans who combined selling beer with the more profitable sale of spirits. Consequently owners of beerhouses resorted to adulteration of their liquor in order to sell at a sufficiently low price, and permitted every kind of disorderly conduct on their premises in order to attract and keep sufficient custom. (Lord Asquith).

Setting the dogs at the bull

1835 Baiting was abolished. The keeping of any house, pit, or other place for baiting or fighting any bear, bull, dog, or other animal was forbidden. So after centuries the sport ceased to rank amongst the amusements of all classes of English people.

1836 Bottled Irish porter (Guinness) outrivalled the London produce, even in London where it was first brewed.

1839 Limitation of Hours Act: public houses in London were closed from midnight on Saturday until noon on Sunday, because there was more drunkenness during those 12 hours than in the whole of the rest of the week.

1840 3rd Beerhouse Act: licences were only to be granted to true resident-occupiers.

1842 Licensing Act: made the transfer of licences easier. Magistrates were empowered to have transfer sessions, and to endorse an existing licence so that the new publican could carry on the business. Known as a 'Protection Order' (sometimes as a 'temporary authority') it would be confirmed at the next full Brewster Session. This system is still in use today.

1844 Charles Wolf and Charles Engles set up a brewery in Philadelphia, and within a year were producing 3,500 barrels.

1845 Gaming Act: disqualified full licencees who allowed billiards in their saloons on Sunday, Christmas Day, or Good Friday.

The tax on glass was rescinded making bottling cheaper.

Carlsberg started brewing lager in Denmark with yeast brought from Munich.

1847 Sugar was permitted in brewing; it provided additional fermentable material and was a means of varying the flavour. Although it had been used previously, its use was now legalized.

1849 Cock fighting was abolished. This Order was exceptionally hard to control as it was a very popular working-class sport, and fights were held in many pubs. It disappeared from the pubs but went on in the fields. Hundreds of thousands of pounds worth of birds – a great many belonging to the poorer classes – could not be destroyed at the Government's whim.

1850 Tax on sugar used in brewing increased, varying from 1/4d to 6/6d a cwt according to quality.

1851 The Maine Liquor Law (USA) introduced by the Mayor of Portland, forbade the public sale of intoxicating drinks. Many English Temperance movements started organizing similar legislation in this country under the auspices of United Kingdom Alliance.

1852 Copyhold Act, when all land was compulsorily registered; pubs can be dated definitely from this time.

1853 The Forbes Mackenzie Act for the better regulation of public houses, fixed 11pm as the hour of closing, and differentiated between grocers who had a certificate to sell liquor for consumption off the premises, and publicans who were prohibited from selling groceries.

Sunday closing was introduced in Scotland.

1855 The 1854 Act was amended slightly making the pubs close from 3pm to 5pm instead of from 2.30pm to 6pm, and making a final closing 11pm instead of 10pm.

These two Acts caused a drop of 4 million gallons in the annual consumption of spirits in the following year.

1860 Refreshment and Wine House Act: Gladstone, as Chancellor of the Exchequer, reduced import duties on wine, especially the lighter kind. One purpose of the Act was to re-unite the business of eating with that of drinking from which, by a fatal error, it had been separated.

1862 Public House Amendment Act: to make more effective the control of the sale of excisable liquors without a licence. In the absence of contrary evidence any place was a shebeen which was 'by repute kept as a shebeen, or in which at the time charged, there were utensils and fittings usually found in Licensed Houses'; the powers of the police were extended. The Act prevented the hawking of liquor, etc.

Church of England Temperance League founded.

1863 Revenue Act: gave those holding 'Beer dealer's licences permission to obtain a further Licence for retailing beer off the premises'.

1869 Wine and Beer House Act consolidated the licences issued by the Excise and made all licences subject to the control of the Magistrates. The beer-houses still paid their licences on production of a certificate from the Magistrates who could not deny the certificates except in special circumstances.

A similar certificate was necessary to obtain a licence to sell beer or wine 'off sales'.

1870 There were 133,840 licensed brewers in England and Wales, but from then on the number started to decline.

There was 1 beerhouse per 182 head of the population: a new Bill proposed that in towns there should be 1 for a population of 1,500 or less, 2 for a population of up to 3,000 and 1 extra for every additional 1,000 people. In the country the Bill proposed 1 for the first 900 people and 1 extra for every additional 600 people. If Magistrates wished to exceed this quota they had to put it to the vote of the ratepayers, who could veto their decision.

1872 A minor Act concerning adulteration of beer was passed. A schedule of deleterious ingredients was issued with heavy penalties for using or having such ingredients on the premises. The ingredients were:

> Cocculus indicus, Chloride of sodium or common salt, Copperas, opium, Indian Hemp, Strychnine, tobacco, darnel seed, extract of logwood, salts of zinc or lead, alum and any extract or compound of the above ingredients.

1874 Pure Beer Act was passed by the Manx Parliament and is still in force: 'no ingredient other than malt, hops and sugar are to be used in brewing.' If found guilty, the brewer is liable to a fine of £300 and the confiscation of his entire plant and stock.

1878 Sunday closing was introduced in Ireland

1879 1st Habitual Drunkards Act: made it illegal to supply liquor to anyone declared to be an habitual drunkard by the Magistrates. Retreats were set up, where alcohol addicts could be treated as voluntary patients, if they paid for their own maintenance. Once in, they could not leave until the cure was finished.

1880 The duty was taken off all materials used in brewing, but was imposed on the specific gravity of the wort; the first rate was 6/3d at a specific gravity of 1057, which was the standard gravity (with a 6% allowance for waste). The measurements were taken by an instrument called a saccharometer. Many small brewers went out of business with the re-introduction of Beer Duty.

1881 Sunday closing in Wales was introduced. Certain areas in Wales are still dry on Sundays; a poll can be taken every 7 years to determine if it is the wish of the district to keep the restriction.

1882 Anders Ohlsson founded the first brewery at Newlands, Cape Province. Lager was first brewed in Britain by the Wrexham Lager Brewery which was founded by 6 Manchester businessmen.

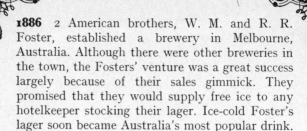

1886 2 American brothers, W. M. and R. R. Foster, established a brewery in Melbourne, Australia. Although there were other breweries in the town, the Fosters' venture was a great success largely because of their sales gimmick. They promised that they would supply free ice to any hotelkeeper stocking their lager. Ice-cold Foster's lager soon became Australia's most popular drink.

1887 Truck Amendment Act, forbade the inclusion of free beer in assessing farm labourers' wages, making farm home-brewing unnecessary.

1888 The coal tar product saccharine was prohibited in brewing on the grounds that it gave an apparent palate to beer equivalent to 4° over its true specific gravity.

1890 Extra duties on beer and spirits were introduced in order to pay compensation to the owners of pubs that were closed by magistrates for reasons other than misconduct by the licensee. (The money raised was in fact allocated to the development of technical education!)

1894 There were 9,664 licensed brewers in Britain.

Beer Tax was increased by 6d a barrel to 6/9d.

1896 Peoples' Refreshment House Association was formed with the Bishop of Chester as Chairman. Its aims were to discourage excessive drinking, to encourage the sale of food and non-intoxicating liquors, and to provide recreation. Its watchwords were good order, cleanliness, reasonable refreshment of all kinds, and comfort for all classes of customer. In 1897 they purchased their first inn – the Sparkford Inn, Sparkford, near Yeovil, Somerset. By the mid-1920s they owned over 170. The Sparkford is now a Bass Charrington House.

1898 2nd Habitual Drunkards Act barred anyone convicted of drunkenness from entering a public house, and made provision for Magistrates to commit criminal inebriates to reformatories.

1900 A mysterious epidemic broke out mainly affecting Salford in Lancashire. It also occurred in other widely-scattered areas. At first it was described as alcoholism or, in some places, multiple neuritis. It affected 6,000 people, 2,000 in Manchester, 500 in Lichfield, and 800 in Salford, and resulted in nearly 70 deaths. Investigation showed that all sufferers were beer drinkers, and that a few of them were employed by the same Salford brewery; suspicion fell upon the beer. Scientists found that sulphuric acid, which was used in producing glucose, could, if slightly contaminated, produce arsenic, which in time entered into the beer. The cause was traced to one particular firm producing glucose and invert sugar for various breweries. There was considerable consternation and alarm throughout the country, but this had died down by the time the Royal Commission report was published in 1903.

Allsops started brewing lager at Burton-on-Trent.

1901 For a total population of 32,528,000 there were 102,000 full 'on' licences.

1904 Compensation Act: the licensee of an alehouse could be refused a renewal of his licence without compensation if he had persistently and unreasonably refused to supply non-alcoholic refreshment at a reasonable price.

The Country Brewers' Society, the London Brewers' Association and the Burton Brewers' Association amalgamated to form the Brewers' Society, which became the national organization for the brewing industry.

1907 31 March: licensed premises were no longer to be used as Courts. Petty Sessions, special Courts, and Coroners' Inquests, had frequently been held in pubs, especially in country areas.

1908 The Children's Act was introduced by Asquith, Chancellor of the Exchequer. It imposed penalties for giving intoxicating liquor to a child

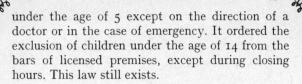

under the age of 5 except on the direction of a doctor or in the case of emergency. It ordered the exclusion of children under the age of 14 from the bars of licensed premises, except during closing hours. This law still exists.

1910 3 August: the Licensing Consolidation Act was introduced by John Simon (later Sir John). It repealed and replaced most of the legislation passed in England and Wales between 1828 and 1906.

1914 King George V closed the Palace wine cellars for the duration of the war, giving a lead to the Nation in those austere times.

1915 Defence of the Realm Act set up the Liquor Control Board in June 1915. It gave wide-ranging powers to restrict drinking in areas where munitions were manufactured by limiting the permitted hours for the sale of alcohol in those areas. Personnel in hospital uniform could not be served, and many licensees were heavily fined for contravening this regulation.

The controls first started in the Lowlands of Scotland, but were extended to other important industrial and shipbuilding areas; by the end of the war, control extended to most of Scotland, England and Wales.

Lloyd George in a speech at Bangor, N. Wales, said, 'Drink is causing more damage in the war, than all the German submarines put together'.

1916 The scheme by which the Government purchased and supplied liquor started in Carlisle. (The Carlisle Brewery was until recently still owned by the Government – it was sold to Theakstones, and the pubs to the tenants and other breweries.)

1919 Volstead Act introduced Prohibition in the USA; brewing on a national scale came to an end until 1933 when the Act was repealed. The alcoholic level was lowered to 3.2% max – equivalent to 1035°. Within 1 year 756 breweries were back in business.

1921 Licensing Act: statutory closing was abolished but hours were limited for consumption 'on' and 'off' to a permitted 9 hours a day in the metropolis, 8½ or 8 hours elsewhere, and 5 hours on Sundays, Christmas Day, and Good Friday except in Wales and Monmouth, where there was no Sunday opening. There must be an interval of not less than 2 hours in the afternoon. Within these hours Magistrates must fix their local permitted hours, with discretion for granting extensions to Houses providing meals, and in areas where there are markets, etc. No credit for drinks was permitted, except where meals were served. The 'long pull' (serving oversized measures, i.e. half-pint into pint) was forbidden.

Barclay Perkins commenced brewing lager.

1923 Intoxicating Liquor Act (Sale to Persons under 18): it became illegal for licensees to sell drink to anyone under 18, with the exception of cider, beer, porter, and perry, which could be sold to anyone over 16, providing it was drunk with a meal.

1931 Snowden's Budget increased the duty on beer from 80/– to 114/– a barrel. The consumption of beer fell from 24 million barrels to 18 million in a year.

1933 First keg beer introduced, by both the Hull Brewery and Watneys.

1934 Magistrates were permitted, at their discretion, to extend closing time from 10pm to 10.30pm for the summer months, mainly for the benefit of farm workers.

1935 December: canned beers were first introduced in Britain by Felinfoil Brewery, Llanelli, S. Wales. It is still an independent brewery with 80 pubs.

1936 453 Registered brewers were in existence in the UK (not including the home breweries).

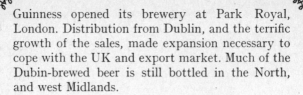

Guinness opened its brewery at Park Royal, London. Distribution from Dublin, and the terrific growth of the sales, made expansion necessary to cope with the UK and export market. Much of the Dubin-brewed beer is still bottled in the North, and west Midlands.

1941 Watneys and Whitbreads gave 25 tons of beer to the beseiged garrison in Tobruk.

1942 20 November: 'Tank'ard week was organized by the licensed trade; the objective was to raise sufficient funds to produce a battalion of tanks. The week was launched on Cambrai Day, which commemorated the day in 1917 when British tanks first penetrated the German lines.

Finance Act enabled licensees of bombed property to suspend their licence without having to apply annually to the Courts or pay an annual licence.

1944 Strong & Co of Romsey supplied the 2nd Tactical Air Force with barrels of beer which were slung in the bomb racks under the wings of new machines that were being flown to airfields in Normandy. The fitting used was known as the XXX Depth Charge Fitment, and was almost passed to the official Modification Committee for registration!

1949 Licensing Act gave Magistrates power to extend hours in London for Houses providing late meals, or music and dancing.

The Budget raised the duty on a standard barrel of beer to a new peak – £364/4½d.

1951 The Brewery Industry Research Foundation was opened at Lyttel Hall, Nutfield, Surrey.

1953 Keg beer, as we know it today, was introduced by Flowers' Luton Brewery. Simond's Tamar Brewery at Devonport had been experimenting with a method of dispensing beer in this manner since World War II, but had given up as they could not supply the beer in good condition.

They dismantled their experimental plant and returned it to Reading. In 1950 a brewery engineer, Mr D. Clarke, visiting the brewery on his half-yearly visit, saw the equipment and listened to the complaints. After 2 years of working at home he perfected and could sell the modern system. Charringtons and Ind Coope soon followed with their own plant, which has now become general, although at least three private breweries have no kegging equipment.

Passenger aircraft allowed to obtain a permit to sell alcohol without need to go through a Magistrates' Court.

The major breweries and many of the minor ones produced Celebration Ales for the Coronation of HM Queen Elizabeth II.

1954 Beer was dropped by RAF patrols to troops in the Malayan jungle at Christmas. One pilot, now on the Brewers' Society staff, dropped 4 bottles of lager in sandbags filled with sawdust to a patrol; 3 bottles landed safely and were much appreciated.

1961 Licensing Act introduced new form of licence for restaurant and residential premises, which must be granted automatically by the Justices, provided the applicant is of good character, and the premises suitable. By 1969 8,000 licences were issued.

Justices were to be more liberal in granting off-licences, taking into greater consideration the convenience to the public, rather than the proof of a need, hence a rapid increase especially in granting of licences to supermarkets.

Licensing Act made provisions for a pub to open and close, within the permitted hours of the area, when the landlord pleased. Most brewery-controlled Houses open and close for the full permitted period, but many Free Houses open later both morning and evening.

10-minute drinking-up time was introduced.

Wales, dry on Sunday for years for religious reasons, was to have a referendum for each region to decide whether to allow Sunday opening. 5 of the 13 counties, together with all 4 county boroughs voted in favour of Sunday opening.

1962 Guinness, Courage, and Scottish and Newcastle Breweries united to launch Harp Lager which is brewed at Courage's Alton Brewery. Ind Coope had launched Skol and Bass Charrington Carling (under licence), but this was the first joint venture by members of the bigger breweries.

1963 Reginald Maudling, Chancellor of the Exchequer, legalized the brewing of beers at home without the necessity of a licence. This soon led to home-brew kits being on sale in the shops.

The Betting and Gaming Act allowed games for small stakes to be played in pubs; games specified were cribbage, dominoes, and certain games of skill, but Magistrates were empowered to add to the list according to local needs.

1967 7 large breweries accounted for 73% of beer production. In order of production they were: Bass, Allied, Whitbread, Watney, Scottish and Newcastle, Courage, and Guinness. Many of them produced beer for a number of personal breweries under their control. The other 27% of beer was produced by 104 breweries.

88 brewery companies owning 160 active breweries were producing approximately 1,500 different varieties of beer; there were also several small breweries (including 5 home-brew houses) which were still in private hands. A total of about 220 breweries in the UK.

The Road Traffic Act 1967 was introduced by Barbara Castle and brought the Breathalyser Test into being.

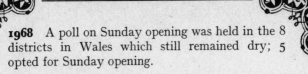

1968 A poll on Sunday opening was held in the 8 districts in Wales which still remained dry; 5 opted for Sunday opening.

1971 Formation of the consumer group CAMRA (Campaign for Real Ale), which has done much to persuade the bigger breweries to stock traditional beer and to serve it traditionally. They have also brought the virtues of such beers to the attention of the general public.

1972 It was recommended that bottle labels be date-stamped like the labels on other long-life foods.

1975 5 September: Lotteries Act was passed enabling clubs registered with local authorities to operate individual lotteries.

1976 27 May: Licensing Amendment Act of England and Wales, relaxing the provisions of the 1964 Act dealing with Special Hours Certificates.

1977 Criminal Act increased considerably the penalties for under-age drinking:

1 Selling intoxicating drinks to anyone under 18: from £25 to £500.
2 Buying intoxicating drinks for a person under 18: from £25 to £200.
3 Buying intoxicating drinks when under 18: from £20 to £200.
4 Refusing to leave licensed premises when drunk: from £5 to £25.

The breweries, except Watneys, Bass, and Scottish and Newcastle, added to the celebrations of the Silver Jubilee by brewing special beers, 55 in all.

1978 Increase in Free Houses in the South of England, mainly because the larger brewers started selling off their unprofitable pubs, which opened up a market for smaller breweries, usually one-man bands producing one brew:

Canterbury Ale, brewed in Moorgate in Flint's sampling room.

Blackawton Bitter, brewed in a small South Devon House near Dartmouth.

Home bitter, brewed behind the old House at Home, Chidham, Sussex.

John Thompson's Special, brewed at Ingleby, Derbyshire.

Lloyd's Country Bitter, brewed by Colin Lloyd.

Porter, brewed at Kempsley, W. Yorkshire.

Porter, brewed at Court Brewery, Herefordshire.

Hawthorne Bitter, brewed at Norfolk House Hotel, Gloucester.

Bourne Valley Bitter, brewed at Walworth, Andover, Hants.

Goose Eye Bitter, Goose Eye, Keighley, Yorks, brewed opposite the pub of that name.

Black Dragon Bitter, brewed at remodelled brewery at rear of Camden Arms.

Butcombe Ale, brewed in a small brewhouse near Frome, Somerset.

Mendip Bitter, Special Bitter, brewed in Cheton, Mendip, Avon.

Nairn Bitter, brewed by a Community Council in Scotland.

1979 The Home Secretary increased the Liquor Licence fee from £6 to £7.50.

On 12 February the Murree Brewery, Rawalpindi, Pakistan (which supplied the author many good pints of traditional ale during the war) closed by Government on religious grounds.

In June the Chancellor increased the tax on beer (by increasing VAT to 15%) by a minimum of 2p a pint on the cheapest, 3p on average and 4p on heavy beers.